Top 10 Baseball Legends

John Albert Torres
AR B.L.: 6.3
Points: 1.0   MG

TOP 10
BASEBALL
LEGENDS

John Albert Torres

Enslow Publishers, Inc.

40 Industrial Road   PO Box 38
Box 398   Aldershot
Berkeley Heights, NJ 07922 Hants GU12 6BP
USA   UK

http://www.enslow.com

Library of Congress Cataloging-in-Publication Data

Torres, John Albert.
    Top 10 baseball legends / John Albert Torres.
        p. cm. — (Sports top 10)
    Includes bibliographical references and index.
    ISBN 0-7660-1493-2
    1. Baseball players—United States—Biography—Juvenile literature.
    [1. Baseball players.] I. Title: Top ten baseball legends. II. Title. III. Series.
GV865.A1 T677   2001
796.357'092'273—dc21

                                    00-010855

Printed in the United States of America

10 9 8 7 6 5 4 3 2 1

To Our Readers: We have done our best to make sure all Internet addresses in this book were active and appropriate when we went to press. However, the author and the publisher have no control over and assume no liability for the material available on those Internet sites or on other Web sites they may link to. Any comments or suggestions can be sent by e-mail to comments@enslow.com or to the address on the back cover.

Illustration Credits: AP/Wide World Photos, pp. 13, 25, 38, 41, 45; Los Angeles Dodgers, Inc., pp. 30, 33; National Baseball Library, Cooperstown, N.Y., p. 37; New York Yankees, p. 18, 35; Pittsburgh Pirates, pp. 6, 9; San Francisco Giants, p. 22; Seattle Mariners/John Cordes, p. 17; Seattle Mariners/Rich Pilling, p. 15; *The Great Baseball Players from McGraw to Mantle* (Mineola, N.Y.: Dover Publications, Inc., 1997), pp. 11, 21, 43; The Oakland Athletics Baseball Company, pp. 27, 29.

Cover Illustration: AP/Wide World Photos.

Cover Description: Mark McGwire.

Interior Design: Richard Stalzer

CONTENTS

Introduction

BASEBALL HAS LONG BEEN CONSIDERED A GAME of statistics. Any sports fan can pick up the local newspaper and quickly find who is leading the league in home runs, batting average, or shutouts.

What about the players who can not be measured with just statistics? What about the players whose careers go beyond batting averages or career totals? What about the players whose greatness goes beyond the baseball diamond? These are the players who have changed the game of baseball. These are baseball legends.

But what exactly makes a baseball legend?

First of all, the most obvious qualification is that he must be a great baseball player. A legend needs to demonstrate that he can achieve greatness throughout long stretches of his career. If the player hits for average, he must hit consistently over .300. If he is a power hitter, he must hit more than thirty home runs a year for several years. A pitcher needs to win twenty games or strike out more than two hundred hitters a season.

Second, a baseball legend must be someone for whom the opposing teams prepare and the fans come out to watch. Hall of Fame pitcher Nolan Ryan was credited with filling baseball stadiums wherever he pitched. Fans knew that something special could happen every time Ryan took the mound. Jackie Robinson would force other teams to change their strategies, especially when he made it to third base. Everyone in the ballpark knew that he could try to steal home.

The third thing that makes a baseball player legendary is that he is credited with changing the game of baseball. These men are larger than life. Perhaps the biggest was Babe Ruth, the Yankees slugger who showed teams that the home run could be a potent offensive tool. He is credited with changing the way hitters approached the art of batting. Instead of slapping at the ball, aiming for holes in the infield, now hitters were swinging from their heels, and going for the fences.

Ask baseball fans who they think are the ten most legendary players of all time and you will get a different list every time. But it would be hard to argue against this list we have put together. On it are representatives of speed, power, pitching, fielding, and hitting—and all have helped shape the game of baseball.

CAREER STATISTICS

Hitter	YR	G	AB	R	H	HR	RBI	SB	AVG
ERTO CLEMENTE	18	2,433	9,454	1,416	3,000	240	1,305	83	.317
COBB	24	3,035	11,434	2,246	4,189	117	1,937	892	.366
GRIFFEY, JR.	12	1,680	6,352	1,163	1,883	438	1,270	173	.296
KEY MANTLE	18	2,401	8,102	1,677	2,415	536	1,509	153	.298
LIE MAYS	22	2,992	10,881	2,062	3,283	660	1,903	338	.302
RK McGWIRE	15	1,777	5,888	1,119	1,570	554	1,350	12	.267
IE ROBINSON	10	1,382	4,877	947	1,518	137	734	197	.311
E RUTH	22	2,503	8,399	2,174	2,873	714	2,213	123	.342
Pitcher	YR	W	L	G	IP	H	BB	SO	ERA
AN RYAN	27	324	292	807	5,386	3,923	2,795	5,714	3.19
YOUNG	22	511	316	906	7,356	7,092	1,217	2,803	2.63

=Years in Majors	HR=Home Runs	L=Losses
;ames Played	RBI=Runs Batted In	IP=Innings Pitched
=At-Bats	SB=Stolen Bases	BB=Bases on Balls (walks)
Runs Scored	AVG=Batting Average	SO=Strikeouts
Hits	W=Wins	ERA=Earned Run Average

ROBERTO CLEMENTE

Roberto Clemente was selected to play in twelve all-star games during his 18-year major-league career.

ROBERTO CLEMENTE

IT WAS NEW YEAR'S EVE 1973. Most people were getting ready to attend parties to welcome in the new year. Roberto Clemente was not like most people. Clemente had heard about an earthquake that had killed thousands of people in the country of Nicaragua. Many people were left without homes. Instead of going to a party, he decided to spend the holiday delivering supplies to that poor country.

His plane to Nicaragua never made it. Shortly after taking off, the plane crashed into the ocean, near San Juan, Puerto Rico. Clemente, one of baseball's biggest stars, was dead.

The Baseball Hall of Fame board of directors decided to overlook the rules. Usually a player has to wait five years after he has stopped playing to make it into the Hall of Fame, but the board immediately voted Clemente in after he died.

"Roberto Clemente belongs in the Hall of Fame," wrote Larry Claflin of the *Boston Herald*. "He belongs there now, not five years from now."[1]

Roberto Clemente was born on August 18, 1934, in Carolina, on the Caribbean island of Puerto Rico. There he played baseball with his friends, even though they sometimes could not afford real equipment. His first bat was made out of a tree branch he found. His first glove was made out of a coffee-bean sack. When there were no real baseballs available, the kids would make one out of a knot of rags.

Clemente was good enough to play in Puerto Rico's professional league when he was a teenager. By the time he was nineteen, the great baseball scout Branch Rickey heard about him. Clemente was a great hitter, runner, and fielder.

Rickey was amazed at Clemente's speed and power. He also had the strongest arm Rickey had ever seen. "Young man," Rickey declared, "you're going to be a superstar."[2] Clemente would join the Pirates in 1955.

In 1960, he started an awesome streak of batting at least .312 for eight straight seasons. He also made the first of his 14 all-star game appearances in 1960 and made it to the World Series that year as well. He collected at least one base hit in every game of the seven-game series against the Yankees, as the Pirates won the world championship.

Over the years Clemente collected many honors and awards. He won 12 consecutive Gold Glove Awards for being the best fielder at his position. He led the league in batting 4 times, and was voted the Most Valuable Player (MVP) in 1966. His strong arm allowed him to throw out runners trying to score. He led the league in outfield assists 5 times.

In 1971, Clemente made the World Series against the Baltimore Orioles his private showcase. He dominated the series, hitting .414 with 12 hits and 2 homers in the seven-game series. He ran the bases with incredible speed. In right field, his rifle-arm cut down several players trying to advance to the next base. The Pirates won another world championship, and Clemente was the Series' MVP. After that series, the country recognized what a great player he had been for many years.

On September 30, 1972, Clemente smashed a double against New York Mets pitcher Jon Matlack. It was hit number 3,000 for Clemente's career. It would also be his last. The superstar died in the plane crash just a few months later.

Famous sportswriter Milton Richman watched Clemente dominate the game for many years. "Only one thing could have really stopped Roberto Clemente, and it did," Richman said after the fatal plane crash.[3]

ROBERTO CLEMENTE

BORN: August 18, 1934, Carolina, Puerto Rico.

DIED: December 31, 1972, San Juan, Puerto Rico.

HIGH SCHOOL: Julio C. Vizcarrondo High School, Carolina, Puerto Rico.

PRO: Pittsburgh Pirates, 1955–1972.

HONORS: National League MVP, 1966; won 12 consecutive Gold Glove Awards; World Series MVP, 1971; elected to Baseball Hall of Fame, 1973 (first Hispanic-American player so honored); became only the second baseball player to be pictured on a United States postage stamp.

After making contact, Clemente sprints toward first base.

Internet Address

http://baseballhalloffame.org/hofers_and_honorees/hofer_bios/clemente_roberto.htm

TY COBB

TY COBB WAS NOT THE MOST WELL-LIKED PLAYER. He was, however, one of the most dominating. Cobb played the game with a fierce determination. Often, Cobb would steal second base and just keep running to third as the catcher was throwing the ball to second.

In 1909, Cobb had what many consider to be the best season in history. The Detroit Tigers outfielder led the league in hitting with a .377 batting average. He was the only player in the league to drive in 100 runs, and he lead the league in home runs—the first player ever to win the Triple Crown of hitting.

Cobb led the Tigers to the 1909 World Series against the Pittsburgh Pirates. Even though the great Pirates won the series in seven games, Cobb showed the country what a great player he was. In Game 2, with the Tigers desperately needing a victory, Cobb found himself on third base in a close game. He had it set in his mind that he would try to steal home against pitcher Vic Willis.

Cobb walked innocently off third base. "I looked harmless," Cobb said. "It was a great moment. . . . he'd left an opening. Just as Willis raised his arm to go into his windup, I broke for the plate with everything I had."[1]

The play was close at the plate, but Cobb executed a perfect hook slide around the catcher, just catching the corner of home plate with his toe. The Tigers went on to have a big inning and won the game easily, 7–2.

Tyrus Raymond Cobb was born December 18, 1886, in Narrows, Georgia. The Cobbs were very poor, even though Ty's father had steady work as a schoolteacher.

TY COBB

Ty Cobb was the first player in baseball history to win the Triple Crown, awarded for leading the league in batting average, home runs, and RBI.

While he was growing up, Ty started playing baseball. His father urged him to quit the "silly" game and get a real job. Ty refused, and the two did not speak to one another for some time. He was determined to make the major leagues and show his father that he could be a success.

Unfortunately, his father did not live long enough to see his son make it to the big leagues. In a tragic accident, Ty's own mother mistook his father for a burglar and shot him to death. The shooting affected Ty deeply.

Cobb bounced back, and was tearing up the amateur league. Players began talking of the young player who would sharpen his baseball spikes and try and knock over opposing players any chance he had.

Cobb was soon patrolling the outfield for the Detroit Tigers. In 1905, he played in 41 games for the Tigers and did not hit much. As a full-time player in 1906, Cobb began an incredible string of batting .320 or better for twenty-three straight years! He led the league in hitting 12 times and even batted better than .400 twice. He was also a great base stealer. In 1915, he stole 96 bases and scored 144 runs. By the time he retired in 1926, he had broken just about every offensive record in baseball. One record that may never be broken is Cobb's lifetime batting average of .367.

Cobb was inducted into the Hall of Fame in 1936. He was the leading vote-getter among the first group of players elected, including Babe Ruth. Despite his reputation as a mean-spirited player, Cobb is still regarded by many as the greatest ever to play the game.

"[He was] greater even than Babe Ruth or Honus Wagner, a unique compelling character . . . an astonishing man who infused such drama, flesh and blood into the chill records he set that his like has not been seen since," said New York *Daily News* sports editor Paul Gallico.[2]

TY COBB

BORN: December 18, 1886, Narrows, Georgia.

DIED: July 17, 1961, Atlanta, Georgia.

HIGH SCHOOL: Franklin County Comprehensive High School, Royston, Georgia.

PRO: Detroit Tigers, 1905–1926; Philadelphia Athletics, 1927–1928.

RECORDS: Highest batting average, career (.366); most runs scored career (2,246); most years (12) and most consecutive years (9) leading the league in batting average.

HONORS: AL Chalmers (MVP) Award, 1911; Triple Crown, 1909; elected to National Baseball Hall of Fame, 1936.

Cobb slides safely into third base. One of the greatest base runners in baseball history, Cobb stole 892 bases during his career.

Internet Address

http://baseballhalloffame.org/hofers_and_honorees/hofer_bios/cobb_ty.htm

KEN GRIFFEY, JR.

KEN GRIFFEY, JR., RACES BACK to the center-field wall. He plants his feet, jumps, and snaps his glove up over the wall, stealing yet another home run from an opposing team. Yet stealing home runs and making circus-type catches is only a small part of Griffey's game. He is one of the most prolific home run hitters in history, with many saying that he will challenge Hank Aaron's record of 755 career round-trippers. He also appears to be a lock to smack out 3,000 hits—the standard by which most great hitters are measured.

"He just keeps moving along, shattering all these records and moving past these famous names, and he's just smiling and having a good time," said former teammate Jay Buhner. "Mr. Consistency. That's him."[1]

Griffey was born on November 21, 1969, in Donora, Pennsylvania. His father, Ken Griffey, Sr., was an all-star player for the Cincinnati Reds and then the New York Yankees. Little Kenny grew up watching his dad play ball, and Junior was allowed to take batting practice with big-leaguers.

He learned to bat in the private batting cage beneath the stands at Yankee Stadium. "That's where he really learned to play the game," said his dad.[2]

By the time he was seventeen, most baseball scouts in America had heard of the young phenom. He was the first player chosen in the June 1987 amateur baseball draft by the Seattle Mariners. His first hit in the minor leagues was a home run.

In less than two years Ken Griffey, Jr., was the starting

Ken Griffey, Jr., lets go of the bat as he begins his home run trot.

KEN GRIFFEY, JR.

center fielder for the Seattle Mariners. In his first major-league at-bat he doubled off ace pitcher Dave Stewart. He was well on his way to winning the Rookie of the Year award when he suffered a broken bone in his hand, causing him to miss a lot of playing time. He finished third in the voting.

At age twenty, Junior, as fans now called him, became the first Mariner ever to start in an all-star game. That same year, Junior and his dad became the first father-and-son combination ever to play on the same team together. On September 14, in a game against the California Angels, the pair combined to hit back-to-back home runs in the first inning.

That season was also Junior's first great defensive season. He became the second youngest player to win a Gold Glove. The next year, Junior made the jump from all-star to one of the game's most dominating players. He broke nearly every Seattle Mariners record by batting .327, slamming 42 doubles, and drawing 21 intentional walks.

By 1993 Junior had become the premier home run hitter in the American League. He belted 45 that year and then a league-leading 40 in 1994. That season, he became the third youngest player ever to reach the 150 home run total. He smacked 56 home runs in both 1997 and 1998.

Besides being a team leader and family man, Griffey spends a lot of his time volunteering with the Make-A-Wish Foundation. "I think he's been very, very moved by some of his experiences with Wish kids," said the Foundation's Cindy Hoppner. "He loves to give. He is a great role model."[3]

Ken Griffey, Jr., is quickly paving himself a way to the Baseball Hall of Fame. One of the greatest players of his time, in 1999 he was voted onto the Major League Baseball All-Century Team.

KEN GRIFFEY, JR.

BORN: November 21, 1969, Donora, Pennsylvania.

HIGH SCHOOL: Moeller High School, Cincinnati, Ohio.

PRO: Seattle Mariners, 1989–1999; Cincinnati Reds, 2000– .

RECORDS: Shares record for most consecutive games with a home run (8); shares postseason single-series record for most home runs (5).

HONORS: Gold Glove Award, 1990–1999; AL MVP, 1997; All-Star game MVP, 1992.

After setting numerous Mariners records, Griffey, Jr., was traded to the Cincinnati Reds prior to the 2000 season.

Internet Address

http://espn.go.com/mlb/profiles/profile/4305.html

MICKEY MANTLE

Taking a long stride, Mantle drives the ball out of the infield. Many considered Mantle to be the greatest switch-hitter the game has ever seen.

MICKEY MANTLE

WHEN MICKEY MANTLE TOOK OVER as the everyday center fielder for the New York Yankees, he replaced all-time great Joe DiMaggio. Yankee fans so loved DiMaggio that they booed Mantle for several years even though he was a great player as well.

Mickey Mantle won a Triple Crown and two MVP awards before he was twenty-six years old. He had incredible speed, was a great fielder, and could hit for a high average. What finally made him a fan favorite was his awesome power.

Mantle hit 536 home runs in a career cut short when he was thirty-six due to injuries and illness. The term "tape measure home run" was invented to measure Mantle's home runs which sometimes traveled more than five hundred feet!

Mantle was born on October 20, 1931, in Spavinaw, Oklahoma. Mickey's dad wanted his son to become a professional baseball player, so he spent a lot of time playing ball with him. He even taught him how to switch hit—batting right-handed against lefty pitchers and batting left-handed against righty pitchers. His father thought being a switch hitter would help Mickey's chances of making it to the big leagues.

While he was a sophomore in high school, Mantle got kicked in the shin and developed a severe infection. Some doctors thought the only way to save him would be to cut off his leg. Mickey's mother took him to another hospital, where they gave him penicillin, and the leg was saved.

Mantle signed a contract with the Yankees after his high

school graduation. Two years later, in 1951, Mantle was standing in right field next to the great DiMaggio. The next season Mickey Mantle was the team's center fielder.

Mantle often hit home runs in important situations. He appeared on 12 World Series teams during his first fourteen years in the majors. He often saved his best play for those championship games and holds the record with 18 World Series home runs.

Even though penicillin saved Mantle's leg, he always had problems with it. In the 1951 World Series, he got his foot caught in a drain chasing a fly ball and tore up his knee. Mantle played in pain almost his entire career.

In 1961, Mantle and teammate Roger Maris were chasing the single-season home run record. It looked as if both players might reach that mark until Mantle went down with an injury. Fans now realized how Mantle endured pain every day and was still a great player.

"He was great, and I wonder and marvel about it," wrote sports commentator Art Rust, Jr. "There has to be something about a man who endured that kind of pain and still came up a winner. I admired his endurance."[1]

During a tremendous career, Mantle made sixteen all-star game appearances, leading the league in home runs four times. Injuries and ill effects from heavy drinking led to an early retirement for this baseball immortal.

After his career was over, Mantle continued to abuse alcohol until 1994, when he decided to enter a rehabilitation clinic and try to quit drinking. Still, all those years of drinking had destroyed his liver. He died at age sixty-three on August 13, 1995.

"He was a presence in our lives—a fragile hero to whom we had an emotional attachment so strong and lasting that it defied logic," said well-known sports announcer Bob Costas.[2]

MICKEY MANTLE

BORN: October 20, 1931, Spavinaw, Oklahoma.

DIED: August 13, 1995, Dallas, Texas.

HIGH SCHOOL: Commerce High School, Commerce, Oklahoma.

PRO: New York Yankees, 1951–1968.

RECORDS: Most times hitting home runs from both sides of the plate in the same game (10); career record for home runs by a switch hitter (536); career record for most home runs in World Series play (18).

HONORS: Triple Crown, 1956; AL MVP, 1956–1957, 1962; Gold Glove Award, 1962; elected to National Baseball Hall of Fame, 1974.

Mickey Mantle was at his best in the most important games. His record for most home runs in World Series play has stood for over thirty-five years.

Internet Address

http://baseballhalloffame.org/hofers_and_honorees/hofer_bios/
mantle_mickey.htm

WILLIE MAYS

Mays has been called the greatest all-around player in
baseball history. He could hit for average and power,
cover a lot of ground in the outfield, throw far and
accurately, and run the bases exceptionally well.

WITH THE CRACK OF THE BAT Willie Mays was gone. His back turned toward home plate, Mays was running full speed toward the center-field fence. As he approached 460 feet deep in center field, he reached up over his right shoulder and caught the ball.

The amazing catch was made even greater when Mays whirled around and threw the ball back to the infield in one motion. His peg held a Cleveland Indians runner from scoring and squashed a potential rally. That catch off the bat of Cleveland slugger Vic Wertz came in the pivotal first game of the 1954 World Series. It is probably the most famous catch in the history of baseball.

Willie Mays, the "Say-Hey Kid," is regarded by many as the most complete player ever to play the game. He did it all. Mays hit for power and average. He stole bases and ran the base paths with reckless abandon. He was also a great fielder.

Mays was not bragging when he was asked to describe himself—he was just being honest. "I think I was the best ballplayer I ever saw," he said.[1] There was not anything he could not do.

William Howard Mays, Jr., was born on May 6, 1931, in Westfield, Alabama, and it seemed as if baseball was in his blood. Willie's father loved baseball too and was a professional player with the Birmingham Black Barons of the Negro Leagues. African Americans were not allowed to play in Major League Baseball until 1947.

Mays played sports all the time as a kid. He not only starred in baseball, but was also a basketball and football star at Fairfax Industrial High School in Birmingham, Alabama. When he was only sixteen years old, Mays already had baseball scouts from the Negro and major leagues following his every move. He signed with the Black Barons in 1947 and then signed a minor-league contract with the New York Giants in 1950.

Mays went through the minor leagues quickly. He was great at every level. The Giants called him up in May 1951. He hit his first home run against future Hall of Famer Warren Spahn. The hit seemed to spark the team, which went into a hot streak after that and made it all the way to the World Series. They lost to their crosstown rivals, the New York Yankees.

After the season, Mays won the first of many awards when he was chosen as the National League Rookie of the Year. Later, the Giants moved to San Francisco and Mays continued to excel. He won two MVP awards and was even named Player of the Decade for the 1960s by *The Sporting News*.

On April 30, 1961, Mays had the game of his life. He cracked four home runs in a single game as the Giants blasted the Milwaukee Braves, 14–4. In all, the Giants hit 8 home runs in the game.

He is third on the all-time home run list with 660 round-trippers. Imagine the numbers Mays would have had if his major-league career was not interrupted by a two-year stint in the army! Mays was a crowd pleaser right up until the day he retired in 1973.

These days he spends time playing golf and assisting the San Francisco Giants in several ways, including working with young players during spring training.

Mays was once asked his approach to playing the game. He responded, "When they throw the ball, I hit it. When they hit the ball, I catch it."[2]

BORN: May 6, 1931, Westfield, Alabama. *79 year old 2008*

HIGH SCHOOL: Fairfield Industrial High School, Birmingham, Alabama.

PRO: Birmingham Black Barons (Negro Leagues); New York/San Francisco Giants, 1951–1952, 1954–1972; New York Mets, 1972–1973.

HONORS: NL Rookie of the Year, 1951; NL MVP, 1954, 1965; Hickok Belt (Pro Athlete of the Year), 1954; All-Star game MVP, 1963, 1968; All-Star game career record for most hits (23); 11-time Gold Glove Award winner; elected to National Baseball Hall of Fame, 1979.

Mays made the all-star team 20 times in his career, each year from 1954 to 1973.

Internet Address

http://baseballhalloffame.org/hofers_and_honorees/hofer_bios/mays_willie.htm

MARK McGWIRE

IT WAS SEPTEMBER 7, 1998, and Busch Stadium in St. Louis was filled to capacity. The game against the Chicago Cubs took on a World Series-like atmosphere. The fans were there for one reason: the home run chase.

Their hero, St. Louis first baseman Mark McGwire, had already cracked 60 home runs during the season. He needed one more to tie the all-time single-season record. He was being chased by Cubs outfielder Sammy Sosa, who had already hit 58 home runs.

McGwire stepped to the plate in the first inning against Cubs pitcher Mike Morgan. On a 2–1 count, Morgan tried to slip a slider by Big Mac. He swung and ripped a tremendous home run to left field.

As he rounded the bases, McGwire high-fived other Cubs. He pointed to the sky and then jumped on home plate, where his son was waiting to greet him. One night later, McGwire hit another home run to break the record. He finished the season with 70 home runs in the most amazing display of power, ever!

Mark McGwire was born on October 1, 1963, in Pomona, California. Mark and his four brothers had a childhood filled with sports. Their father, John McGwire, was a dentist who took up boxing to stay in shape.

All the boys were good athletes, but Mark became an instant baseball star. As a ten-year-old Little Leaguer, Mark belted 18 home runs in thirty games. He went to a Catholic high school, Damien High, and pitched for the school team.

His coach, Tom Carroll, knew that McGwire was also a

In 1987, Mark McGwire set a rookie-record with 49 home runs for the Oakland A's.

MARK McGWIRE

great hitter. When he was not pitching, he usually played the outfield or first base.

McGwire attended the University of Southern California, where he was a star pitcher along with Randy Johnson. McGwire was too good a hitter not to play every day, so by his junior season he moved to first base.

In 1984 McGwire was selected by the Oakland A's in the amateur draft. During the 1987 season he hit a rookie-record 49 homers, and was named Rookie of the Year. He posted very solid numbers during the next five years, helping lead the A's to two World Series appearances. In 1993, a sore left heel limited McGwire to only twenty-seven games. The next season, he experienced a sore back and more heel problems, which kept him to only forty-seven games. The injuries gave him a lot of time to spend in the gym increasing his upper-body strength, and watching videotapes of pitchers.

The next season, 1995, McGwire was finally healthy, and he became an even more dangerous hitter than before. He belted 39 homers that season and then smacked 52 round-trippers in 1996. On July 31, 1997, McGwire was dealt by the rebuilding A's to the St. Louis Cardinals. He smacked 58 home runs that season.

After his record-breaking 70-home run season, McGwire did not slow down. The next year, 1999, he hit 65 home runs and celebrated a milestone by belting career home run No. 500.

The thing that gives McGwire the greatest satisfaction is how he has been supported by the American public. "The way people across America have treated me this year it's almost as if we broke the record together. People told me, 'I can relate to you.' Well, they did because I'm just a normal guy, because I show emotion and because I care about other people, especially children."[1]

MARK McGWIRE

BORN: October 1, 1963, Pomona, California. 52 years old

HIGH SCHOOL: Damien High School, Claremont, California.

COLLEGE: University of Southern California.

PRO: Oakland Athletics, 1986–1997; St. Louis Cardinals, 1997– .

RECORDS: Single-season record for most home runs (70); record for most consecutive seasons with 50 or more home runs; major-league record for most home runs by a rookie (49).

HONORS: *The Sporting News* College Player of the Year, 1984; member of 1984 U.S. Olympic baseball team; AL Rookie of the Year, 1987; Gold Glove Award, 1990; *The Sporting News* Sportsman of the Year, 1997–1998.

The A's traded McGwire to the St. Louis Cardinals during the 1997 season. With the Cardinals, McGwire rewrote the record books, clubbing 70 home runs in 1998.

Internet Address
http://espn.go.com/mlb/profiles/profile/3866.html

JACKIE ROBINSON

In 1947, Jackie Robinson became the first African American to play major-league baseball in the twentieth century. That season, Robinson was named Rookie of the Year.

JACKIE ROBINSON

JACKIE ROBINSON WAS THIRTY-SIX YEARS OLD and nearing the end of his career. Yet there he was, taking a gigantic lead off third base in the 1955 World Series against the New York Yankees. Robinson jumped up and down off third base to try to distract Yankees pitcher Whitey Ford. He broke for home and then stopped, in an effort to ruin Ford's concentration. No one really thought Robinson would steal home. He was not supposed to be that fast anymore.

On the second pitch Robinson took off for home. He arrived at home plate just as the ball did, and he somehow eluded catcher Yogi Berra's tag with a beautiful hook slide. Jackie Robinson had stolen home again. That play helped send a message to his Dodgers teammates not to give up. They eventually won the 1955 World Series, finally beating the Yankees.

Babe Ruth changed baseball—Jackie Robinson changed America.[1] Before 1947, baseball was a lot different than it is today. African-American baseball players were not allowed to play in Major League Baseball.

Jackie Robinson was born in Cairo, Georgia, on January 31, 1919. His father, Jerry, abandoned the family when Jackie was only sixteen months old. His mother, Mallie, was determined to keep the rest of the family together. She moved them to California in 1920.

In California, Mallie had to work several jobs. The family lived in a quiet neighborhood in Pasadena, California. The Robinsons were the only African-American family in the neighborhood, and they became the targets for prejudice and hatred.

Robinson was angry at the way he was treated and found sports to be a good outlet. In high school, he starred in track and field, baseball, football, and basketball. After high school, he went to Pasadena Community College. Soon, UCLA wanted Robinson to enroll so he could star for its teams. Because of his skin color, though, there were few athletic opportunities after graduation.

Robinson served in the U.S. Army during World War II. Next, he decided that he would try out for the Kansas City Monarchs, a Negro League baseball team.

On October 23, 1945, Branch Rickey signed Robinson to a minor-league contract with the Brooklyn Dodgers. He explained to Robinson that the only way to beat racism was not to fight back and argue. "The only way for a black man to break the color line is not to retaliate. Not to answer a blow with a blow or a curse with a curse," said Rickey.[2]

In April 1947, Jackie Robinson was twenty-eight when he became the first African-American player in the twentieth century to compete in a major-league baseball game.

Robinson was named the 1947 Rookie of the Year by *The Sporting News*. He then won the National League MVP award in 1949. He was selected to play in the all-star game each year from 1949 to 1954. Most important, Robinson opened the door for other African-American players to cross the color line and play major-league baseball.

He was elected to the Baseball Hall of Fame in 1962. When he retired, Robinson became a spokesman for civil rights. He died on October 24, 1972.

In 1997, baseball retired Robinson's number, forty-two, from every baseball team. In a tribute to Jackie Robinson, no one will ever again wear his number.

JACKIE ROBINSON

108 years old 2008

BORN: January 31, 1919, Cairo, Georgia.

DIED: October 24, 1972, Stamford, Connecticut.

HIGH SCHOOL: Muir Technical High School, California.

COLLEGE: Pasadena Junior College, Pasadena, California; UCLA.

PRO: Kansas City Monarchs (Negro Leagues); Brooklyn Dodgers, 1947–1956.

RECORDS: First African-American player to play in Major League Baseball.

HONORS: NL Rookie of the Year, 1947; NL MVP, 1949; NL batting crown, 1949; led NL in stolen bases, 1947, 1949; elected to National Baseball Hall of Fame, 1962.

Over the course of his ten-year career, Robinson stole home an incredible 19 times.

Internet Address
http://baseballhalloffame.org/hofers_and_honorees/hofer_bios/robinson_jackie.htm

BABE RUTH

BABE RUTH, THE GREATEST HOME RUN HITTER of his time, stepped up to bat in the 1932 World Series. Cubs fans, and players themselves, stood up and started yelling at him trying to make him lose concentration.

The first pitch was a strike, and the fans and players went wild. Ruth smiled at them and held up one finger as if to say "That's only strike one." He did the same thing after strike two was called. Now, Ruth smiled even more widely and pointed to the outfield bleacher seats. Was he saying that he would hit a home run there?

Chicago pitcher Charlie Root yelled at Ruth to get back in the batter's box. He pitched the ball, and Ruth hit a tremendous home run, right in the area that he had pointed to. As usual, the Yankees, led by the great Babe Ruth, swept the World Series in four games.

George Herman Ruth, Jr., was born on February 6, 1895, in Baltimore, Maryland. He grew up in a very poor, rough section of the city. His parents did not spend much time with him, and George, whose nickname was Babe, rarely went to school. He often just found himself getting into trouble hanging out on the city streets.

When he was seven years old, he was placed in the St. Mary's Industrial School, a reform school for boys who were constantly getting into trouble. It became Ruth's new home—and he loved it.

There were eight hundred boys enrolled and many participated in sports. By the time he was eighteen, Ruth was known as the best baseball player in the school. Everyone talked about his monstrous home runs.

BABE RUTH

Babe Ruth was one of the best pitchers in baseball when his contract was sold to the New York Yankees. With the Yankees, Ruth's power hitting revolutionized the game.

In 1914, Ruth signed a minor-league contract with the Baltimore Orioles of the International League. Five months later, the Boston Red Sox bought out his contract and made Ruth a pitcher. Within two years he was a twenty-game winner. In the 1916 and 1918 World Series, he pitched 29²/₃ scoreless innings, a record that stood until 1961.

In 1919, the owners of the Red Sox made one the worst moves in baseball history. They sold Ruth to the New York Yankees, who made him an outfielder. Within two seasons, Ruth changed the game. He introduced raw power to baseball.

In 1920, Ruth hit 54 home runs for the Yankees. Only one other entire team managed to hit 50 home runs for the season. In 1921, he set a new record with 59 round-trippers. In 1927, as part of a Yankees lineup that was dubbed Murderer's Row, Ruth blasted 60 home runs. That record stood until 1961.

Ruth led the league in homers 12 times. He also led the league in runs batted in 6 times and in runs scored 8 times. He led the Yankees to seven World Series appearances and helped them win 4 times. He finished his career with a whopping 714 home runs. Yankee Stadium later became known as "The House that Ruth Built."

Babe Ruth was known as a colorful character who loved life and who loved children. He often partied with his teammates, and spent a lot of time visiting with sick children in hospitals. In one famous story, Ruth was said to have promised a dying boy that he would hit a home run for him. He wound up hitting three!

Famous sportswriter Jimmy Cannon described Babe Ruth as a national treasure. "Babe Ruth was a parade all by himself, a burst of dazzle and jingle. . . . Babe Ruth made the music that his joyous years danced to in a continuous party. . . . What Babe Ruth is, comes down, one generation handing it to the next, as a national heirloom."[1]

BABE RUTH

BORN: February 6, 1895, Baltimore, Maryland. *124 years old 2008*

DIED: August 16, 1948, New York, New York.

HIGH SCHOOL: St. Mary's Industrial School for Boys, Baltimore, Maryland.

PRO: Boston Red Sox, 1914–1919; New York Yankees, 1920–1934; Boston Braves, 1935.

RECORDS: Most home runs by left-handed batter (714); most years leading the league in home runs (12); single-season record for most runs scored (177); single-season record for most walks (170); single-season record for highest slugging percentage (.847) and career (.690).

HONORS: AL MVP, 1923; elected to National Baseball Hall of Fame, 1936.

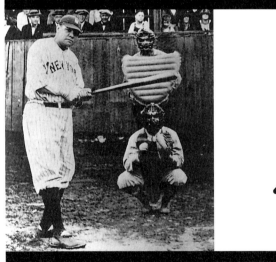

Over the course of his career, Ruth led the American League in home runs 12 times.

Internet Address

http://baseballhalloffame.org/hofers_and_honorees/hofer_bios/ruth_babe.htm

NOLAN RYAN

Ryan overcame control problems early in his career to become one of the most dominating pitchers in the 1970s and 1980s.

BY THE START OF THE 1973 SEASON, many knew that Nolan Ryan was a hard-throwing right-handed pitcher. He struck out an awful lot of people but also struggled with control. Then on May 15, he joined baseball's immortals by pitching a no-hitter against the Kansas City Royals. While the buzz of Nolan Ryan's name was still fresh, Ryan made baseball headlines again.

It was July 15, and Ryan knew from the start of the game that he had his special fastball—which came to be known as the Ryan Express. He was throwing the ball much faster than 90 miles per hour. It would be a long day for the Detroit Tigers. They struck out 17 times against Ryan and did not get a base hit. He had pitched two no-hitters in the same season.

Lynn Nolan Ryan was born on January 31, 1947, in Refugio, Texas. Ryan played high school baseball at Alvin High School, in Alvin, Texas, where word of his dominating fastball spread quickly. Although Ryan's control problems and skinny frame kept him from getting drafted out of high school, he began attracting attention pitching for Alvin Junior College.

In 1965 the New York Mets selected Ryan in the eighth round of the amateur draft. Scout Red Murff saw beyond the skinny body and the wild throws.

"I appreciate the fact that Red spent so much time with me and worked with me to help me become a better pitcher," Ryan said.[1]

In 1966, Ryan dominated the minor leagues. He won 17 games and struck out 272 batters. By 1968 he was a regular in the Mets starting rotation. He posted a 6–9 record but also struck out 133 batters in 134 innings. The next season he posted similar numbers, working as a starter and relief pitcher for the 1969 World Series champions.

By 1972, the Mets felt Ryan was not progressing as quickly as they would have liked, so they traded him to the California Angels. That was the move that changed Ryan's career. "I like to refer to my years with the Angels as the foundation for my career," he would later say.[2]

Coaches in California worked with Ryan to make his windup and delivery shorter. Immediately he became a better pitcher. In 1973, Ryan struck out a record 383 batters. In 1974, Ryan struck out over 300 batters for the third straight season, and pitched his third no-hitter.

On August 20, 1974, Ryan again made it into the record books. He became the first hurler to have his fastball clocked at over 100 miles per hour. In 1975, Ryan pitched his fourth no-hitter.

For the next few seasons Ryan was the dominant pitcher in the American League. Still, the Angels rarely had a good ballclub, and Ryan wanted to be closer to his wife and children. In 1980, Ryan signed a contract with the Houston Astros.

He pitched the next fourteen seasons with the Astros and the Texas Rangers. In 1989, Ryan struck out 301 batters, making him, at forty-two years old, the oldest pitcher ever to strike out 300 men.

By the time his amazing career was over, Ryan had won 324 games, pitched a record 7 no-hitters, and struck out a record 5,714 batters. Some feel his strikeout record will never be broken.

NOLAN RYAN

BORN: January 31, 1947, Refugio, Texas.

HIGH SCHOOL: Alvin High School, Alvin, Texas.

COLLEGE: Alvin Junior College, Alvin, Texas.

PRO: New York Mets, 1968–1971; California Angels, 1972–1979; Houston Astros, 1980–1988; Texas Rangers, 1989–1993.

RECORDS: Career record for most no-hitters (7); career record for most strikeouts (5,714); single-season record for most strikeouts (383); career record for most seasons played (27).

HONORS: *The Sporting News* Man of the Year, 1990; elected to National Baseball Hall of Fame, 1999.

Throughout his career Ryan was well known for exercising during the offseason to stay in top physical shape. This allowed him to play for 27 seasons, a major-league record.

Internet Address

http://baseballhalloffame.org/hofers_and_honorees/hofer_bios/ryan_nolan.htm

CY YOUNG

ON AUGUST 13, 1908, ALL AMERICAN LEAGUE baseball games were postponed for the day. Instead, an all-star team faced the Boston Red Sox and ace pitcher Cy Young.

The all-star team faced the world's best pitcher and his teammates as a tribute. Within one hour of being announced, the game was sold out. Young pitched the first two innings of the exhibition and then was honored by the American League and opposing teams. It was quite a tribute for a player who had yet to retire.

Cy Young was not an ordinary superstar. He was arguably the greatest baseball pitcher who ever played the game. Today, the best pitcher in each league is awarded the Cy Young Award for pitching excellence.

Denton True Young was born on March 29, 1867, in Gilmore, Ohio. He grew up on a farm and spent much of his time doing chores. Whenever he had free time, Young would play baseball.

In 1890, a scout spotted the twenty-three-year-old Young throwing a baseball against a fence. Legend has it that the fence looked as if a cyclone had smashed it. Soon after that, Young was known as Cyclone or Cy. The scout signed him to a contract with the Canton ballclub of the Tri-Sate League. At the time, this was almost equal to today's minor-league baseball teams. He won a respectable 15 games for Canton. Still, only one big-league team showed interest in him: the lowly Cleveland Spiders of the National League.

He made his major-league debut for the Spiders on August 6, 1890, pitching a three-hitter against the Chicago

Many feel that Cy Young's record of 511 wins will never be broken.

CY YOUNG

White Stockings. The Spiders won, 8–1. Young never looked back.

Young used two pitches, a blazing fastball and sinker, to post a decent 9–7 record during his rookie season. The next year, however, Young posted 27 victories and started a string of fourteen seasons with at least nineteen wins. He won more than thirty games in a season five different times.

Cleveland struggled to win year after year, so they decided, in 1899, to trade Cy to St. Louis. In 1900, Young won only 19 games, and some people thought that the thirty-three-year-old was finished. Then, he joined Boston of the American League and won 33 games that season and 32 the following year.

On May 5, 1904, Young pitched the finest game of his career when he threw a perfect game against the Philadelphia Athletics. A perfect game occurs when a pitcher does not allow a single base runner in the game. Twenty-seven hitters come to bat, and all twenty-seven are retired.

"Of all the 879 games I pitched in the big leagues," Young said of his perfect game, "that one in Boston stands clearest in my mind."[1]

Although Young led the major leagues in victories only once in his career, nobody has ever come close to his amazing career statistics. He pitched 751 complete games, pitched 7,356 innings, and won an astonishing 511 games. His lifetime earned run average was 2.63.

Sometimes Young would pitch on only one or two days' rest. When he retired after the 1911 season, he said that he had never experienced a sore arm in his life.

Young was elected to the Hall of Fame in 1937. He spent the last years of his life quietly on his farm and died on November 4, 1955.

Born: March 29, 1867, Gilmore, Ohio.

Died: November 4, 1955, Newcomerstown, Ohio.

Pro: Cleveland Spiders, 1890–1898; St. Louis Cardinals, 1899, 1900; Boston Red Sox, 1901–1908; Cleveland Indians, 1909–1911; Boston Braves, 1911.

Records: Career record for most wins (511).

Honors: Annual Cy Young Award for pitching excellence named in his honor; elected to the National Baseball Hall of Fame, 1937.

Young was elected to the Hall of Fame in 1937 as part of the Hall's second class.

Internet Address

http://baseballhalloffame.org/hofers_and_honorees/hofer_bios/young_cy.htm

CHAPTER NOTES

Roberto Clemente

1. Samuel Regaldo, *Viva Baseball* (Chicago: University of Illinois Press, 1998), p. 153.

2. Terry Egan, Stan Friedmann, and Mike Levine, *The Macmillan Book of Baseball Stories* (New York: Macmillan Books, 1992), p. 33.

3. Regaldo, p. 148.

Ty Cobb

1. Al Stump, *Cobb* (Chapel Hill, N.C.: Algonquin Books of Chapel Hill, 1994), p. 179.

2. Ibid., p. 96.

Ken Griffey, Jr.

1. Tom Verducci, "Joltin' Junior," *Sports Illustrated*, May 17, 1999, p. 34.

2. Ken Griffey, "My Son, the Ballplayer," *Sports Illustrated*, June 21, 1999, p. 29.

3. Susan Wade, "More than a Game: Ken Griffey, Jr., Makes Kids' Wishes True," *Seattle Mariners Official Web Page*, August 6, 1999, <http://www.mariners.org/players/k_griffey/griffey_feature_080699.asp> (February 22, 2000).

Mickey Mantle

1. Art Rust, Jr., *Legends: Conversations with Baseball Greats* (New York: McGraw-Hill Publishing Co., 1989), p. 136.

2. Larry Schwartz, "Mantle Was First in Fans' Hearts," *ESPN SportsCentury*, n.d., <http://espn.go.com/sportscentury/features/00016135.html> (February 22, 2000).

Willie Mays

1. "Quotations from Willie Mays," *Baseball Almanac—Quotations*, 2001, <http://www.baseball-almanac.com/quomays.shtml> (May 10, 2001).

2. Larry Schwartz, "Mays Brought Joy to Baseball," *The Baseball Page—San Francisco Giants*, n.d., <http://www.sportsdogg.com/san_francisco_giants.htm> (May 10, 2001).

Mark McGwire

1. Mark McGwire with Tom Verducci, "Where Do I Go from Here?" *Sports Illustrated*, September 21, 1998, p. 52.

Jackie Robinson

1. Mike Shatzkin, *The Ballplayers* (New York: Arbor House Publishers, 1990), p. 927.

2. Joshua Hanft, *Jackie Robinson* (New York: Baronet Books, 1991), p. 145.

Babe Ruth

1. Daniel Okrent and Harris Levine, *The Ultimate Baseball Book* (Boston: Houghton Mifflin Company, 1981), p. 143.

Nolan Ryan

1. Nolan Ryan, "Transcript of Nolan Ryan's Speech," *Induction Speeches*, July 25, 1999, <http://www.baseballhalloffame. org/hof_weekend/1999/speeches/ryan_nolan.htm> (February 22, 2000).

2. Ibid.

Cy Young

1. "Yesteryear: Cy Young," *Boston Red Sox Official Home Page*, n.d., <http://www.redsox.com/yesteryear/legends/young.htm> (February 22, 2000).

INDEX

A
Aaron, Hank, 14
B
Baltimore Orioles, 8, 36
Birmingham Black Barons, 23
Boston Red Sox, 36, 42
Brooklyn Dodgers, 31
Buhner, Jay, 14
C
California Angels, 16, 40
Cannon, Jimmy, 36
Carroll, Tom, 26
Chicago Cubs, 26, 34
Clafin, Larry, 7
Clemente, Roberto, 6–9
Cleveland Indians, 23
Cleveland Spiders, 42
Cobb, Ty, 10–13
Costas, Bob, 20
D
Detroit Tigers, 39
DiMaggio, Joe, 19
F
Ford, Whitey, 31
G
Gallico, Paul, 12
Griffey, Jr., Ken, 14–17
Griffey, Sr., Ken, 14
H
Hoppner, Cindy, 16
Houston Astros, 40
I
International League, 36
J
Johnson, Randy, 28
K
Kansas City Monarchs, 32
Kansas City Royals, 39
M
Mantle, Mickey, 18–21
Maris, Roger, 20
Matlack, Jon, 8

Mays, Willie, 22–25
McGwire, Mark, 26–29
Milwaukee Braves, 24
Morgan, Mike, 26
Murff, Red, 39
N
Negro Leagues, 23, 24, 32
New York Giants, 24
New York Mets, 8, 39
New York Yankees, 8, 14, 19, 24, 31, 34, 39
P
Philadelphia Athletics, 44
Pittsburgh Pirates, 8
R
Richman, Milton, 8
Rickey, Branch, 7–8, 32
Robinson, Jackie, 4, 30–33
Root, Charlie, 34
Rust, Jr., Art, 20
Ruth, Babe, 4, 10, 31, 34–37
Ryan, Nolan, 4, 38–41
S
St. Louis Cardinals, 28
Seattle Mariners, 14, 16
Sosa, Sammy, 26
Spahn, Warren, 24
Stewart, Dave, 16
W
Wagner, Honus, 12
Wertz, Vic, 23
Willis, Vic, 10
World Series, (1909), 16
  (1916), 36
  (1918), 36
  (1932), 34
  (1951), 20, 24
  (1954), 23
  (1955), 31
  (1960), 8
  (1969), 40
  (1971), 8
Y
Young, Cy, 42–45